Words
Cross & Across

Words
Cross & Across
Word Search on Barack Obama

COMPILED BY DR. EUGENE WILLIAMS, SR.

First Edition 2008

Cover photo courtesy: *Obama for America*

ISBN: 978-0-615-26292-5

Academic Resources Unlimited, Incorporated
P .O. Box 6745, Washington, D.C. 20020
(301) 768-8316
educationissues@hotmail.com

SOME BOOKS ON BARACK OBAMA

- *Barack Obama*
  by Barack Obama
- *The Audacity of Hope:*
  Thoughts on Reclaiming the American Dream
  by Barack Obama
- *Barack Obama: An American Story*
  by Roberta Edwards
- *Hopes and Dreams: The Story of Barack Obama*
  by Steve Dougherty
- *Barack Obama In His Own Words*
  by Lisa Rogak
- *Barack Obama: The New Face Of American Politics*
  by Keith Boeckelman
- *Barack Obama*
  by John K. Wilson
- *Barack Obama*
  by Heather Lehr Wagner

Acknowledgments

What an adventure it has been assembling this unique, one of a kind word search book! Compiling it could not have been completed without the assistance and support of my students, high school and college, who appeared to be most interested in seeking words that describe the Obamas. They even got me more intrigued about word searches and charts like those included in this book. They strengthened my faith in Barack's capability to become the President of US and his ability to serve as a good role model, a great communicator whom I pray they will all emulate. Family encouragement and support always mean a lot to creative people. Therefore, I acknowledge my wife who offered that smile of support when I mentioned what I wanted to do, my son, a wordsmith and author, along with his wife, Jewel and my beautiful, smart granddaughter, Paige. Also Myka, my basketball star granddaughter and her mother, Imelda who challenged me once to complete a publication that would appeal to a vast market. Thanks for the challenge, Imelda.

My university students at Southeastern University are to be commended and acknowledged for their response to the first word searches given to them on Barack & Michelle. They conducted exhaustive research on the topic, "Perceptions of Barack Obama" and posted a questionnaire on *youtube.com*. They also agreed to give a word search on Barack to each respondent to the questionnaire. Fahim Munshi of International Graphics, my printer, gave me useful suggestions based on his experience as a marketing communications professional. Maggie Wong, one of my university students, provided outstanding support with the word charts and word searches as did Nicholas Scott, one of my gifted high school students.

Note to the Word Seeker

Teachers, parents, and young people, do you like words? Do you want to improve your knowledge of Barack Obama and move your vocabulary to another level and emulate Barack Obama? I know you have noticed how articulate and eloquent this young leader is. Well, you can improve your vocabulary by engaging in the word searches here in this class and family related guide. Moreover, you can become as word smart as Barack, for he is, indeed, one of the most distinguished orators in the United States. Some liken him to Abraham Lincoln, Dr. Martin Luther King, Jr., Senator John Kerry, and a host of other great speakers. One reason they are great speech makers is that they have extensive vocabularies that they use well. Word searches and word charts in this book contain commonly used and SAT type words that will serve the word seeker well in speaking and writing. This book may be used by teachers to expose their children to President Obama and to improve their word knowledge and usage. To assess the understanding of the words, parents can develop simple tests. Please don't pass up this opportunity to make our children more literate and successful in writing, conversations, and on standardized tests. I sincerely want you to have as much fun and learn as many new words as I did in completing this much needed material. Let the art of oral and written communication thrive.

Note to Teachers and Mentors

As a high school and university English teacher, I have learned that too many of our students have limited vocabularies, which is one thing that separates them from the majority culture student and from corporate America. Often many of our most gifted students in mathematics and other related areas feel intimidated around children from a more advantaged population. Their vocabularies are too restricted. This vocabulary achievement gap will increase if teachers, elementary through high school don't find innovative ways to deal with vocabulary deficiency among our students. I think I have at least one answer for improving vocabulary. It evolved from a classroom experience at an alternative high school in Maryland. During Black History Month 2008, I focused the celebration on two very famous Black, eloquent men–Dr. Martin Luther King, Jr. and Senator Barack Obama. Students were required to read the "I Have A Dream" speech by Dr. King and Chapter 6, 'Faith' from *The Audacity of Hope* by Senator Obama. We read these pieces of literature aloud as we all know the value of reading aloud.

Many of my students experienced difficulty pronouncing some of the vocabulary. I just assumed they had this problem because they were not taught in elementary school how to phonetically pronounce words.

When I asked them to define words such as "cynic", they did not know the definitions, but they were anxious to learn. I have never met a student who did not want to learn new vocabulary words, whether they used them after learning them or not. I have had tremendous success in inspiring both university and high school students to learn and use effective words in their writing and speaking. I was determined to get their students to pronounce and define some of King's and Obama's words.

First, I designed a word chart like the one in this guide. Students began developing such charts using www. dictionary.com and the dictionary. They liked developing their charts and using the words they learned in sentences. Of course, some had more success than others. All were required to produce charts culminating in group or one-on-one discussing of the words.

After I saturated them with word charts, I required them to make word searches of the words learned and to share them with classmates and even with their parents. We did searches on Julius Caesar and The Great Gatsby. I knew I was headed for success with another word learning approach.

At that point, I decided to do word charts and word searches on Barack Obama. I believe they know as much about him from the charts and searches as they would have learned from reading a book about him. I believe you will too, upon going through this book.

Word study the way I used to teach it can be boring for most students. The approach that I'm offering is not just a memory approach (lowest level of Bloom's Taxomy but application is the highest level) but one that teaches the knowledge and application of new words around a very significant historian figure, Senator Barack Obama.

Since it has and will continue to work for me as an effective teaching approach, I am certain it will work for you as well.

Contents

	Puzzle	Solution
The Obamas: A Friendly Family	11	121
Barack's Wife: Michelle Obama	15	122
Barack's Older Daughter: Malia Obama	19	123
Barack's Younger Daughter: Sasha Obama	23	124
Barack's Mother: Ann Dunham	27	125
Barack's Maternal Grandmother: Madelyn Dunham	31	126
Barack's Maternal Grandfather: Stanley Dunham	35	127
The Orator	39	128
The Audacious Man	43	129
The Intellectual	47	130
The Powerful Man	51	131
The Decisive Man	55	132
A Man Embracing Change	59	133
A Man of Faith	63	134
The Determined Man	67	135
The Loquacious Man	71	136
The Peace Maker	75	137
An Honest Man	79	138
The Resourceful Man	83	139
Making Things Go Well and Being Kind	87	140
The Positive Force	91	141
The Kind, Friendly Man	95	142
The Luminous Man	99	143
Recreation	103	144
The Intelligent Man	107	145
A Sociable Man	111	146
A Physical Man	115	147

Barack Obama's
Victory Speech
Page149

The Obamas

A Friendly Family

"Happy families are all alike, every unhappy family is unhappy in its own way."

– Leo Tolstoy

THE OBAMAS: A FRIENDLY FAMILY

```
i y n o m r a h l e
t l y c o r d i a l
l d a a t a r m l b
o n o i t c e f f a
g e n i a l l y m c
y i l i b a t i l i
a r y a i i a b n m
m f f n m b c d b a
a f e a l l a i e a
a g l e e y o e r i
```

AFFABLE   AFFECTION   AMIABLE
AMICABLE   AMITY   FRIENDLY
GENIAL   GENIALLY   CORDIAL
HARMONY

(Solution on page 121)

13

THE OBAMAS: A FRIENDLY FAMILY

WORD	DEFINITION	SENTENCE
Affable	pleasantly easy to approach and to talk to	He is an **affable** and courteous gentleman.
Affection	fond attachment, devotion, or love	The lovely baby wins everyone's **affection.**
Amiable	having or showing pleasant, good-natured personal qualities	The host is always **amiable** to the visitors.
Amicable	characterized by or showing goodwill; friendly; peaceable	The dispute ended in an **amicable** settlement.
Amity	friendship; peaceful harmony	
Friendly	characteristic of or befitting a friend; showing friendship	He gave us a **friendly** greeting.
Genial	diffusing warmth and friendliness	He is a **genial** host.
Genially	in an affable manner	He **genially** treated us during our visit.
Cordial	showing warm and heartfelt friendliness	He gave us a **cordial** welcome.
Harmony	a harmonious state of things in general and of their properties	They worked in perfect **harmony**.

Barack's Wife
Michelle Obama

*"A wife is essential
to great longevity;
she is the receptacle of
half of man's cares, and
two-thirds of his ill-humor."*
– Charles Reade

BARACK'S WIFE: MICHELLE OBAMA

```
a  mi  a  b  l  e  e  g
r  l  l  t  t  e  a  r  s
d  a  n  s  t  a  a  p  r
e  i  f  a  n  d  a  e  e
n  n  d  f  a  a  y  n  l
t  e  e  m  a  w  i  s  b
s  g  a  n  a  b  a  i  u
t  n  b  l  u  e  l  v  l
t  n  e  u  q  o  l  e  o
r  a  l  u  g  n  i  s  v
```

ARDENT   ELOQUENT   AFFABLE
LAWYER   GENIAL   ADAMANT
SEDATE   PENSIVE   SINGULAR
VOLUBLE   AMIABLE

(Solution on page 122)

Words, Cross & Across

BARACK'S WIFE: MICHELLE OBAMA

WORD	DEFINITION	SENTENCE
Ardent	characterized by strong enthusiasm	She is an ardent admirer of the ballet.
Eloquent	expressing yourself readily, clearly, effectively	He is an eloquent speaker.
Affable	diffusing warmth and friendliness	She gave us an affable smile.
Lawyer	a professional person authorized to practice law; conducts lawsuits or gives legal advice	He is a famous lawyer.
Genial	diffusing warmth and friendliness	The woman is so genial that she will make friends wherever she goes.
Adamant	not capable of being swayed or diverted from a course; unsusceptible to persuasion	She is adamant to temptation.
Sedate	dignified and somber in manner or character and committed to keeping promises	She is a sedate and graceful girl.
Pensive	persistently or morbidly thoughtful	The woman in this painting has a pensive smile.
Singular	unusual or striking	She is a singular woman.
Voluble	marked by a ready flow of speech	She is an extremely voluble young woman.
Amiable	diffusing warmth and friendliness	He impressed them as a modest and amiable young man.

Barack's
Older Daughter
Malia Obama

"A daughter is one of
the most beautiful gifts
this world has to give."
– Laurel Atherton

BARACK'S OLDER DAUGHTER: MALIA OBAMA

```
e t c u r i o u s h
v h e u i v o d b a
i o a l r i u c i m
t u c b b v u e o i
c g e l b a r o d a
a h m i t c c b u f
a t e v u i i i a a
r f h p h o t f m t
l u f i t u a e b a
u l p o i s e d v u
```

ACTIVE   CURIOUS
BEAUTIFUL   ADORABLE
POISED   THOUGHTFUL
VIVACIOUS   AMICABLE

(Solution on page 123)

BARACK'S OLDER DAUGHTER: MALIA OBAMA

WORD	DEFINITION	SENTENCE
Active	characterized by energetic activity	She is an active toddler.
Curious	eager to investigate and learn or learn more	She is curious about everything.
Beautiful	delighting the senses or exciting intellectual or emotional admiration	This is a beautiful woman.
Adorable	lovable especially in a childlike or naive way	What an adorable child!
Poised	in full control of your faculties	She is perfectly poised and sure of herself.
Thoughtful	acting with or showing thought and good sense	You're very thoughtful.
Vivacious	vigorous and active	She is a vivacious and charming hostess.
Amicable	characterized by friendship and good will	In consideration of the amicable relationship between us, we are willing to hold further negotiation with you.

Barack's
Younger Daughter

Sasha Obama

*"There are only
two lasting bequests
we can give our children.
One is roots, the other wings."*

–Hodding Carter

BARACK'S YOUNGER DAUGHTER: SASHA OBAMA

```
c u r i o u s d r l s
d q e l b a r o d a p
e i e u e e d m h d o
r i f f d e s i o p l
e v i t i s i u q n i
a y f h a l e r t o t
d p e g n b i t r l e
e p r u t o i k o c n
r a m o r o u s i p b
s h d h s a i n u n n
l i i t a e m e p e d
```

INQUISITIVE   AMOROUS   ADORABLE
NICE   KIND   POISED
ALERT   HAPPY   CURIOUS
POLITE   THOUGHTFUL   OBEDIENT
READER

(Solution on page 124)

BARACK'S YOUNGER DAUGHTER: SASHA OBAMA

WORD	DEFINITION	SENTENCE
Inquisitive	showing curiosity	She is inquisitive about everything.
Amorous	inclined toward or displaying love	She is an amorous idealist.
Adorable	lovable especially in a childlike or naive way	What an adorable child!
Nice	pleasant or pleasing or agreeable in nature or appearance	We had a nice time at the party.
Kind	having or showing a tender and considerate and helpful nature; used especially of persons and their behavior	She is always kind to other people.
Poised	in full control of your faculties	She is perfectly poised and sure of herself.
Alert	very attentive or observant	We must be alert enough to spot the opportunity when it comes.
Happy	enjoying or showing or marked by joy or pleasure or good fortune	She gave us a happy smile.
Curious	eager to investigate and learn or learn more	She is curious about everything.
Polite	showing regard for others in manners, speech, behavior, etc.	What a polite and well-behaved child!
Thoughtful	acting with or showing thought and good sense	You're very thoughtful.
Obedient	dutifully complying with the commands or instructions of those in authority	She is an obedient little girl.
Reader	a person who enjoys reading	She is a fast reader .

Barack's Mother

Ann Dunham

"Mother's love is the fuel that enables a normal human being to do the impossible."

– Marion C. Garretty

BARACK'S MOTHER: ANN DUNHAM

```
a c f r q r q e f k r a d l r
n p i a p q e r w e q r e a e
v b x t u z i h h m h w n e s
p b m y s e r c t z o t i n o
u h q l n i r e a o h c m j l
r f b d d a l k t r m c r f u
c k l j e a z a o w b c e n t
g y b s t w e p e w u c t h e
d j e p n a o s z d t f e d t
n r z g h l c o r a i n d j e
b t u i o p t i m i s t i c i
t e n g i l l e t n i y y d u
t r i f j l q e z u e u x n q
w s r e m a e r d l r h t g h
t w q v y w d b g j n n n i y
```

MOTHER

TACITURN

INTELLIGENT

DREAMER

IDEALISTIC

DETERMINED

QUIET

RESEARCHER

OPTIMISTIC

RESOLUTE

ANTHROPOLGIST

FRIENDLY

(Solution on page 125)

BARACK'S MOTHER: ANN DUNHAM

WORD	DEFINITION	SENTENCE
Mother	a woman who has given birth to a child (also used as a term of address to your mother)	She is the mother of two little girls.
Quiet	free of noise or uproar; or making little if any sound	She is a quiet woman.
Taciturn	habitually reserved and uncommunicative	She is a taciturn person.
Researcher	a scientist who devotes himself to doing research	The researcher wants to blend the substance in with the others.
Intelligent	having the capacity for thought and reason especially to a high degree	What is the most intelligent animal in the universe?
Optimistic	expecting the best	She is very optimistic .
Dreamer	someone guided more by ideals than by practical considerations	She was dismissed as a dreamer .
Resolute	firm in purpose or belief; characterized by firmness and determination	They stood resolute against the enemy.
Idealistic	of high moral or intellectual value; elevated in nature or style	Ironically, sometimes the most idealistic decisions can yield the most practical gains.
Anthropologist	a social scientist who specializes in anthropology	The anthropologist transcribed the sentences of the native informant.
Determined	devoting full strength and concentrated attention to	He is a determined fighter of the God.
Friendly	characteristic of or befitting a friend	She is a friendly person.

Barack's Maternal Grandmother

Madelyn Dunham

"To reform a man, you must begin with his grandmother."

– Victor Hugo

BARACK'S MATERNAL GRANDMOTHER: MADELYN DUNHAM

```
e a g e e t b t t r f
c t r n m p r n d n p n
t n a h i r s e t s r c
e n n n h r o e a a o t
e r d t o r a r t m t e
e m m h e i t c p f e t
v s o h l u s e i l c m
y h t r o w t s u r t o
n o h r b e c t a o i m
m w e g n a s e s p v r
g t r t l s n g i n e b
a e a i v g e k e i p t
```

CARING   COMPETENT
FISCAL   BANK
MOTHER   PASSIONATE
PROTECTIVE   TRUSTWORTHY
GRANDMOTHER   BENIGN

(Solution on page 126)

Words, Cross & Across

BARACK'S MATERNAL GRANDMOTHER: MADELYN DUNHAM

WORD	DEFINITION	SENTENCE
Caring	to feel concern about	He doesn't care what others say.
Fiscal	of or pertaining to financial matters in general	a fiscal policy of incurring budget deficits to stimulate a weak economy
Mother	a female parent	She is his mother
Protective	having the quality or function of protecting	a protective covering
Grandmother	the mother of one's father or mother	She is his grandmother.
Competent	having suitable or sufficient skill, knowledge, experience, etc., for some purpose; properly qualified	He is perfectly competent to manage the bank branch.
Bank	a long pile or heap; mass	a bank of earth; a bank of clouds
Passionate	having, compelled by, or ruled by intense emotion or strong feeling; fervid	a passionate advocate of socialism
Trustworthy	deserving of trust or confidence; dependable; reliable	The treasurer was not entirely trustworthy
Benign	showing or expressive of gentleness or kindness	showing or expressive of gentleness or kindness

34

Barack's Maternal Grandfather
Stanley Dunham

*"To my great-grandfather,
I owed the advice to dispense
with the education of the schools
and have good masters at home
instead–and to realize that no
expense should begrudged
for this purpose."*

– Victor Hugo

Words, Cross & Across

BARACK'S MATERNAL GRANDFATHER: STANLEY DUNHAM

```
u y t n a i l a v a m
s l d g a f a t h e r
h d c t n m y u e d f
t n e i l i s e r a l
h e g s t b m e n y e
e i d c a e g r l c m
l r a n s e g l a a e
p f d e n c c r n h s
f r p l a c i e e r c
u e e a i n r e d n c
l d n i g t a e r e e
```

RESILIENT   HUSBAND   VALIANT
FATHER   FRIENDLY   CARING
DECEASED   CHARMING   HELPFUL
ENERGETIC   SALESMAN

(Solution on page 127)

37

BARACK'S MATERNAL GRANDFATHER: STANLEY DUNHAM

WORD	DEFINITION	SENTENCE
Resilient	recovering readily from adversity, depression, or the like	She is very resilient to changes.
Husband	a married man; a woman's partner in marriage	She worshiped her husband .
Valiant	having or showing valor	It was a valiant attempt.
Father	a male parent (also used as a term of address to your father)	Everyone has a father .
Friendly	characteristic of or befitting a friend	The instructor gave me a friendly warning.
Caring	showing a care	Children need a caring environment.
Deceased	someone who is no longer alive	They wept for the deceased .
Charming	pleasing or delighting	She is a charming girl.
Helpful	providing assistance or serving a useful function	You've been very helpful .
Salesman	a person employed to sell merchandise	He is a humorous salesman.

Barack Obama

The Orator

"There is no true orator
who is not a hero."

– Ralph Waldo Emerson

BARACK OBAMA: THE ORATOR

```
r i e o e e o r i e e k
r h a r l e b e p c p h
s p e a k e r k s l p s
h s k t e k e a p e e i
e r k i o a i e i r n a
p p m o s r f p h r k h
r f i n a i i s e e m k
s r e k a m h c e e p s
s a h p k s c i i i r b
e r e a a s e l c a i r
s n c r i e e b r e n s
o h e s h e p u a k r b
r s s n t n s p e e c h
```

SPEAKER   ORATION
SPEECH   PUBLIC SPEAKER
RHETORICIAN   SPEECHMAKER
SPEECHIFIER

(Solution on page 128)

BARACK OBAMA: THE ORATOR

WORD	DEFINITION	SENTENCE
Speaker	someone who talks (especially someone who delivers a public speech or someone especially garrulous)	Who's the next **speaker?**
Oration	an instance of oratory	He gave us an inspiring **oration.**
Speech	the act of delivering a formal spoken communication to an audience	He is artfully persuasive in his **speech.**
Public speaker	a person who delivers a speech or oration in public	Clarity of diction is vital for a **public speaker.**
Rhetorician	a person who delivers a speech or oration	Abraham Lincoln was one of the greatest American **rhetoricians.**
Speechmaker	a person who delivers a speech or oration	Martin Luther King was one of the greatest American **speechmakers.**
Speechifier	a person who delivers a speech or oration	Abraham Lincoln was one of the greatest American **speechifiers.**

Barack Obama

The Audacious Man

"If men knew all that women think, they would be twenty times more audacious."

– Alphonse Karr

BARACK OBAMA: THE AUDACIOUS MAN

```
b a a c s n n n b a e o
e o s l b m d d n r a n
s h l b r a s h n e s s
r a c d a c y i n c b d
g d e i v a r d d n r a
y t i r e m e t i e a r
y p n e f b t d p d s i
a s s u r a n c e i h n
s s e n d l o b r f n g
g e m o s e r u t n e v
v e o r y c f n n o s i
c l r n s s f r i c s t
d a u n t l e s s d n n
```

BOLD   TEMERITY
ASSURANCE   BRASHNESS
GALL   EFFRONTERY
BRAVE   CONFIDENCE
BRASHNESS   BOLDNESS
DARING   VENTURESOME
DAUNTLESS   INTREPID

(Solution on page 129)

45

Barack Obama: The Audacious Man

WORD	DEFINITION	SENTENCE
Bold	Fearless and daring	You are exceedingly bold.
Temerity	Audacity	He had the temerity to call me a liar.
Self-Assurance	Freedom from doubt: belief in yourself and your abilities.	I'm lack of self-assurance.
Brashness	The trait of being rash and hasty	I'm very annoyed at your brashness .
Gall	A feeling of deep and bitter anger and ill-will	When you taste honey, remember gall.
Effrontery	Audacious (even arrogant) behavior that you have no right to	The politician had the effrontery to ask the people he had insulted to vote for him.
Confidence	Having or marked by confidence or assurance	He is a politician full of confidence.
Boldness	The trait of being willing to undertake things that involve risk or danger	The proposal required great boldness.
Daring	Disposed to venture or take risks	He is a daring aviator.
Venturesome	Involving risk or danger	She is a venturesome investor.
Dauntless	Invulnerable to fear or intimidation	Dauntless in spirit, they became stronger through hardship.
Intrepid	fearless	He is not really satisfied with his intrepid action.
Brave	Possessing or displaying courage; able to face and deal with danger	A brave retreat in a brave exploit.

Barack Obama

The Intellectual

"To do nothing at all is the most difficult thing in the world, the most difficult and the most intellectual."

– Oscar Wilde

BARACK OBAMA: THE INTELLECTUAL

```
g n i e i d l s a i e u
n o a e r d e i m e r a
i s t e s i s n u a a n
d a i t s e i n i a r b
n e d u c a t e d a a t
a r t n n e n n c e r a
t n e g i l l e t n i b
s d l i u m t l t t a r
r l e c n t c n e i e a
e c n e g i l l e t n i
d s c h o l a r s n n n
n i c e r e b r a l l i
u m t n e i b e b m u g
```

INTELLIGENT   SMART
REASON   UNDERSTANDING
INTELLECT   BRAIN
INTELLIGENCE   BRAINED
MIND   BRAINIER
BRAINIEST   EDUCATED
SCHOLAR   CEREBRAL

(Solution on page 130)

49

BARACK OBAMA: THE INTELLECTUAL

WORD	DEFINITION	SENTENCE
Intelligent	having the capacity for thought and reason especially to a high degree	Can you say that dolphins are much more **intelligent** than other animals?
Smart	showing mental alertness and calculation and resourcefulness	It is easy to teach **smart** students.
Reason	the capacity for rational thought or inference or discrimination	There's a great deal of **reason** in his advice.
Understanding	the capacity for rational thought or inference or discrimination	His **understanding** of English is very good.
Intellect	knowledge and intellectual ability	His **intellect** embraces every field of science.
Brain	mental ability	He is the **brains** of the company.
Intelligence	the ability to comprehend; to understand and profit from experience	People vary in **intelligence.**
Brained		He is a **mad-brained** young man.
Brainlessly	not using intelligence	He acted **brainlessly.**
Cerebral	involving intelligence rather than emotions or instinct	It's a **cerebral** approach to the problem.
Mind	an important intellectual	He is a man with a **mind** of the first class.
Educated	possessing an education (especially having more than average knowledge)	He is an **educated** man.
Scholar	a learned person	He is an accomplished **scholar.**
Brainy	having or marked by unusual and impressive intelligence	Some men **dislike** brainy women.

Barack Obama

"Nearly all men can stand adversity, but if you want to test a man's character, give him power."

– Abraham Lincoln (1809 -1865)

BARACK OBAMA: THE POWERFUL MAN

```
g n e a o n r g n t
g n i l l e p m o c
t y i m g n l n r g
t g t n a s s i u p
m g a h g t n e o l
h n n g g i i t i n
t i e s l i e p l n
e l e i i n m r g n
n u p u t a n r e n
n r t n t t c m g g
```

MIGHTY   RULING
REIGNING   COMPELLING
POTENT   REGNANT
PUISSANT

(Solution on page 131)

53

BARACK OBAMA: THE POWERFUL MAN

WORD	DEFINITION	SENTENCE
Mighty	having or showing great strength or force or intensity	He is a **mighty** orator.
Ruling	exercising power or authority	At that time, nobility is the **ruling** class of the society.
Reigning	exercising power or authority	The terror that is **reigning** across Indonesia is making everyone fearful.
Compelling	driving or forcing	Everyone sees it as **compelling** to align technology policy with business policy.
Potent	having the power to influence or convince	Beauty is potent, but money is more **potent**.
Regnant	exercising power or authority	Orange is the **regnant** colour of this summer.
Puissant	powerful	The famous cathedral is really grave and **puissant**.

Barack Obama

The Decisive Man

"Character, in the long run, is the decisive factor in the life of an individual and of nations alike."

– Theodore Roosevelt

Barack Obama: The Decisive Man

```
e t u l o s e r o u t f
v t i i v f v g s a l i
i e i t s p i r a u r u
t u o t o l t m i f v t
a i t t l i a v p n u f
c u p g t m t i t o i i
i a c c i c l c i r f
f o t i a s r r i u i t
i u r t r v o u f l r v
n i a o a r h e r u i c
g i t n v g t i r c i o
i i i t a e u s t l i i
s a s u e n a i i t v o
```

RESOLUTE   **CRUCIAL**
OF IMPORT   **SIGNIFICATIVE**
AUTHORITATIVE

(Solution on page 132)

BARACK OBAMA: THE DECISIVE MAN

WORD	DEFINITION	SENTENCE
Resolute	firm in purpose or belief	He stood **resolute** against the enemy.
Crucial	of extreme importance	It is a **crucial** issue for women.
Of Import	of great significance or value	He is a man **of import**.
Significative	pointing out or revealing clearly	This letter is **significative** of her affection.
Authoritative	having authority or ascendancy or influence	The captain's manner is **authoritative.**

Barack
Obama
A Man Embracing Change

*"The universe is change;
our life is what our
thoughts make it."*
– Marcus Aurelius Antoninus

Barack Obama: A Man Embracing Change

```
n l x c s q a y g o d y l g n
a o q y w o l j s y f h h q l
k c i n o i t a c i f i d o m
s n t t l q e f d o x u o g z
l d e i a i r o b n o c n g l
l p y u o r m r e v i s e g y
s n f b h n e n m i r g w s f
r o x a y r q t a y a n o v d
h i f f c m x t l z n u f o c
n s y y n s i w m a r z w i g
m i v x c f a n e r x i j l t
p v m l x x m e x o u m j m h
h e j g x z b f b n m d d g p
w r z w r l b g u j p e v a x
w h l h s w n x r x a x l g e
```

ALTERATION   **ACTION**
MODIFY   **ALTER**
MODIFICATION   **REVISION**
REVISE

(Solution on page 133)

BARACK OBAMA: A MAN EMBRACING CHANGE

WORD	DEFINITION	SENTENCE
Alteration	the act of revising or altering	The **alterations** to your coat will take a week.
Action	something done	**Actions** speak louder than words.
Modify	cause to change; make different; cause a transformation	The equipment may be **modified** to produce VCD sets.
Alter	cause to change; make different; cause a transformation	These clothes are too large; they must be **altered.**
Modification	the act of making something different	The law, in its present form, is unjust; it needs **modification.**
Revision	the act of revising or altering (involving reconsideration and modification	The books would benefit by further **revision.**
Revise	the act of making something different	I've been **revising** the book all week.

Barack
Obama

A Man of Faith

*"Faith is a continuation
of reason."*

– William Adams

BARACK OBAMA: A MAN OF FAITH

```
s c t g a e c a c l a
s n o e c s a e a e r
e s o m l a i t c i n
n t i i m e t n a i o
l s a t g i a y i b i
u c o m m i t m e n t
f a f m g i l l m r a
h n o e l c i e u a c
t c l e c e o s r f i
i l d b f b t t n t d
a i a l a l f f e t e
f t l l i r e a i i d
```

TRUST BELIEF

RELIGION FAITHFULNESS

FIDELITY ALLEGIANCE

COMMITMENT DEDICATION

COMMITTAL COMMIT

(Solution on page 134)

65

BARACK OBAMA: A MAN OF FAITH

WORD	DEFINITION	SENTENCE
Trust	have confidence or faith in	**Trust** me!
Belief	any cognitive content held as true	We should respect other people's **belief**.
Religion	a strong belief in a supernatural power or powers that control human destiny	I am a person without **religion**.
Faithfulness	the quality of being faithful	One of his virtues is **faithfulness**.
Fidelity	the quality of being faithful	She praised the servant for his **fidelity**.
Allegiance	the loyalty that citizens owe to their country	His **allegiance** has never been questioned.
Commitment	the trait of sincere and steadfast fixity of purpose	He is a man of energy and **commitment**.
Dedication	complete and wholehearted fidelity	His talent and **dedication** will insure his success.
Committal	the official act of consigning a person to confinement	She articulated her strong **committal** to world peace.
Commit	give entirely to a specific person, activity, or cause	She **committed** herself to the work of god.

Barack Obama

The Determined Man

"The path to success is to take massive determined action."

– Anthony Robbins

BARACK OBAMA: THE DETERMINED MAN

```
c r u n d i s c o u r a g e d
o u n w a v e r i n g u d c a
u d f e l e b t d a e e d s u
r i a e e r s s e l r a e f a
a n l e t u l o s e r t v i f
g t t e n u n v d a h a l t v
e d e t n u a d n u i u o n e
o v r l u d e s e a n u s e v
u g i l b g t a t t t t e b i
s u n s h a k a b l e k r - s
l e g s l t d l d a n r b l i
s n e w t u t n d r t a r l c
g e a d n e p f e l i o e e e
n r s d u a a m g b o v i h d
t a d e s s e d o a n b e d g
a r u g t d r l y c t u b n b
```

RESOLUTE
COMPULSIVE
DECISIVE
UNFALTERING
UNWAVERING
STALWART
UNDETERRED
INTENTION
UNBENDABLE
FEARLESS

DRIVEN
COURAGEOUS
UNSHAKABLE
HELL-BENT
RESOLVED
UNDAUNTED
UNDISCOURAGED
STEADFAST
STEADY

(Solution on page 135)

Barack Obama: The Determined Man

WORD	DEFINITION	SENTENCE
Resolute	firm in purpose or belief	He is **resolute** for peace
Driven	urged or forced to action through moral pressure	He feels a **driven** sense of obligation to speak for his people.
Compulsive	caused by or suggestive of psychological compulsion	**Compulsive** drinking is bad for one's health.
Courageous	possessing or displaying courage; able to face and deal with danger or fear without flinching;	He has quiet a reputation for being **courageous.**
Decisive	determining or having the power to determine an outcome	He gave a **decisive** answer.
Unshakable	determining or having the power to determine an outcome	It is our **unshakable** policy to help them to do that.
Unfaltering	marked by firm determination or resolution; not shakable	With **unfaltering** determination, it should be possible to resolve the housing problem
Hell-bent	recklessly determined	He is **hell-bent** on having his own way
Unwavering	marked by firm determination or resolution; not shakable	He is **unwavering** in devotion to friend.
Resolved	determined	He **resolved** to work harder
Stalwart	dependable	He is a **stalwart** supporter of UN.
Undaunted	unshaken in purpose ;resolutely courageous	He continued the climb, **undaunted** by the severe storm.
Steady	Not subject to change or variation especially in behavior	It's important for the stock market to stay **steady**.

70

Barack Obama

The Loquacious Man

"He who seldon speaks, and with one calm well-timed word can strike dumb the loquacious, is a genius or a hero."

– Johann Kaspar Lavater

BARACK OBAMA: THE LOQUACIOUS MAN

```
d l e h y g e a e d e e e
e e a i h a v b e l y t a
h h i t a r i h g t o b y
t t g l c r t a l k y i r
u d k m k u a t u l c a t
o g g d o l k a s h u m h
m o a m a o l b a g r g m
r r g b t u a t u u d s i
e i u b b s t g e a r e b
b b a r a y o m r t e b v
b b a b e g o s y a c a u
a u l g b m a v m a u u t
l b b l h e l a l b h y a
b u a b d r g t h r g l a
```

CHATTY   GABBY
GARRULOUS   TALKY
TALKATIVE   BLABBER MOUTHED
BIGMOUTHED

(Solution on page 136)

73

BARACK OBAMA: THE LOQUACIOUS MAN

WORD	DEFINITION	SENTENCE
Chatty	prone to friendly informal communication	He's a friendly **chatty** sort of person.
Gabby	full of trivial conversation	She was kept from her housework by **gabby** neighbors.
Garrulous	full of trivial conversation	A woman, especially a **garrulous** old one, is very annoying.
Talky	full of trivial conversation	My son is very **talky** sometimes.
Talkative	friendly and open and willing to talk	My husband is an extremely **talkative** person.
Blabber Mouthed	someone who gossips indiscreetly	She was kept from her housework by the **blabber mouthed** neighbor.
Bigmouthed	full of trivial conversation	She was kept from her housework by **bigmouthed** neighbors.

Barack Obama

The Peace Maker

*"Peace is not merely
a distant goal that we seek,
but a means by which
we arrive at that goal."*

– Martin Luther King, Jr.

Barack Obama: The Peace Maker

```
p g s p p t y a l m h e i
e e m y a l l a o i c r c
a i y i f l i l v i i o l
c g o l t i l e i l e t i
e t a i l i c n o c t a g
f d a l f u g a e c a c h
u e e y l f f a p p c i t
l s e a c e s e t t a f e
e a i v v i v s c e l i n
a e p r e i f i c a p c t
s p r o p i t i a t e a t
e p p ml e l i c t e p l
d a s s u a g e r a e i t
s w e e t e n l r r p l p
```

PEACEFUL   PEACEFULLY   PACIFICATOR
PACIFY   MOLLIFY   PACIFIER
PACIFIC   APPEASED   ASSUAGER
PLACATE   SWEETEN   CONCILIATE
PROPITIATE   RELIEVE   ALLAY
EASED   MITIGATE   LIGHTEN
ALLEVIATE

(Solution on page 137)

BARACK OBAMA: THE PEACE MAKER

WORD	DEFINITION	SENTENCE
Peaceful	not disturbed by strife or turmoil or war	We all want a **peaceful** world.
Peacefully	in a peaceful manner	The reform was brought into effect **peacefully**.
Pacify	fight violence and try to establish peace in (a location)	The U.N. troops are working to **pacify** Bosnia.
Appeased	cause to be more favorably inclined; gain the good will of	The angry passenger was **appeased** by their apology.
Assuage	cause to be more favorably inclined; gain the good will of	She managed to **assuage** the angry customer.
Placate	cause to be more favorably inclined; gain the good will of	He never attempts to **placate** his enemy.
Sweeten	make sweeter, more pleasant, or more agreeable	He always tries to **sweeten** his family life.
Conciliate	cause to be more favorably inclined; gain the good will of	I managed to **conciliate** with my mom.
Propitiate	make peace with	They offer a sacrifice to **propitiate** the god.
Relieve	alleviate or remove	He **relieved** from the pressure and the stress of work.
Allay	lessen the intensity of or calm	The news **allayed** my conscience.
Eased	made easier to bear	Talking **eased** his anxiety.

Barack Obama

An Honest Man

"Honesty is the first chapter in the book of wisdom."

– Thomas Jefferson

BARACK OBAMA: AN HONEST MAN

```
d o o d r e h r d s u p c
n n a e r e c n i s n s h
d l s p s r d r n e p b s
c o u e r s f p b l r i e
r h o n o r a b l e e u a
o t i d t u o r l l t u u
t d c a d r u e b i e a s
t e a b t r u a e u n l a
b a r l i t i t r g t o n
r f e e e l u t h b i l g
o h v c e a u e t f o l u
e t a r u c c a a v u r p
n a e i r e b e e s s l a
```

UNPRETENTIOUS   UNTRUTHFUL
VERACIOUS   HONORABLE
RELIABLE   DEPENDABLE
GUILELESS   SINCERE
TRUE   ACCURATE

(Solution on page 138)

BARACK OBAMA: AN HONEST MAN

WORD	DEFINITION	SENTENCE
Unpretentious	lacking pretension or affectation	This is an **unpretentious** country church.
Untruthful	not expressing or given to expressing the truth	The statement given under oath was **untruthful.**
Veracious	habitually speaking the truth	He is such a **veracious** boy.
Honorable	not disposed to cheat or defraud; not deceptive or fraudulent	His conduct speaks him **honorable.**
Reliable	worthy of being depended on	The news is **reliable.**
Dependable	worthy of reliance or trust	Our wares are always **dependable.**
Guileless	free of deceit	She gave him a **guileless** look, but he knew he couldn't really trust her.
Sincere	open and genuine; not deceitful	Please accept my **sincere** apologies.
True	consistent with fact or reality; not false	The story is **true.**
Accurate	conforming exactly or almost exactly to fact, or to a standard or performing with total accuracy	He is consistently **accurate.**

Barack Obama

The Resourceful Man

"The truly successful person inspires others to do more than they have thought possible for themselves."

– Denis Waitley

BARACK OBAMA: THE RESOURCEFUL MAN

```
t e f e t e a d
n n e e t d a n
e t a u q e d a
d c t n e c a f
i i t a b p f t
f c o d d e d t
n d n a e n t a
o e q f e p a d
c a p a b l e p
```

**CAPABLE   CONFIDENT
ADEQUATE**

(Solution on page 139)

85

BARACK OBAMA: THE RESOURCEFUL MAN

WORD	DEFINITION	SENTENCE
Capable	having capacity or ability	He is **capable** of judging art.
Confident	having or marked by confidence or assurance	We are **confident** of success.
Adequate	enough to meet a purpose	The supply is not **adequate** to the demand.

Barack Obama

Making Things Go Well & Being Kind

"A kind and compassionate act is often its own reward."

– John William Bennett

Words, Cross & Across

BARACK OBAMA:
MAKING THINGS GO WELL AND BEING KIND

```
s r b b f i l e e g r e
r i e e e e e d n e n n
e o n r e o t f b n k t
h e t f n g i n e b i r
t e e c i i g e n f o n
o l e e a e n o e h i e
g s e d h f n n v p b s
n h r t s e e d o n c i
i n t i n b n n l i b a
p n e s o e i i e e e o
l i n r o b e k n b h e
e n b l f b a s t n s e
h l n n b i n s s t n d
```

BENEFACTOR   BENIGN
BENEFIT   HELPING OTHERS
BENEVOLENT   KIND

(Solution on page 140)

Barack Obama: Making Things Go Well and Being Kind

WORD	DEFINITION	SENTENCE
Benefactor	a person who helps people or institutions especially with financial help)	We need as many **benefactors** as possible for the victims of the catastrophe.
Benign	pleasant and beneficial in nature or influence	She is a **benign** old lady.
Benefit	something that aids or promotes well-being	He is always warmhearted in public **benefits**.
Helping others	contributing to the fulfillment of a need or furtherance of an effort or purpose	Sometimes **helping others** means to sacrifice some of your own benefits.
Benevolent	intending or showing kindness	The teacher taught us to be **benevolent**.
Kind	having or showing a tender and considerate and helpful nature	He is a very **kind** person.

Barack Obama

The Positive Force

"Optimism is essential to achievement and it is also the foundation of courage and true progress."

– Nicholas Murray Butler

BARACK OBAMA: THE POSITIVE FORCE

```
a m g y l d n e i r f t n t e
g l c k c r e d i b l e m r l
e a l i i e x c i m h q c u b
n c e u t n e g i l i d o s a
t b l y r e d j j s y i h t r
l s d l n i g h i b i v e w o
e t r e l a n r e k w v r o n
k n o w l e d g e a b l e r o
v i v a c i o u s n r e n t h
a m b i t i o u s m e t t h n
t a l e n t e d g d i v e y a
l u f e c a e p a c u l j d i
g n i t a l u m i t s o i r p
t s a f d a e t s x s o r n v
d a z z l i n g o a b n j p g
```

AMBITIOUS	**DILIGENT**	**FRIENDLY**
ENERGETIC	**CALM**	**COHERENT**
CREDIBLE	**ALERT**	**ALLURING**
DAZZLING	**DECISIVE**	**PROUD**
SMILING	**STEADFAST**	**GENTLE**
HONORABLE	**KINDHEARTED**	**KNOWLEDGEABLE**
PEACEFUL	**STIMULATING**	**TALENTED**
TRUSTWORTHY	**VIVACIOUS**	

(Solution on page 141)

BARACK OBAMA: THE POSITIVE FORCE

WORD	DEFINITION	SENTENCE
Alert	mentally responsive	He is alert and thoughtful.
Calm	steadiness of mind under stress	He usually stays calm.
Dazzling	amazingly impressive; suggestive of the flashing of lightning	What a dazzling piece of work it is!
Energetic	possessing or exerting or displaying energy	The more the young students worked, the more energetic they became.
Honorable	showing or characterized by honor and integrity	He is an honorable man.
Likeable	easy to like; agreeable	He is an attractive and likeable young man.
Smiling	smiling with happiness or optimism	He is popular because of his smiling face.
Talented	showing a natural aptitude for something	You are so talented .
Alluring	highly attractive and able to arouse hope or desire	I couldn't resist his alluring smile.
Coherent	marked by an orderly, logical, and aesthetically consistent relation of parts	The government needs a coherent economic policy.
Decisive	characterized by decision and firmness	We need a decisive leader.
Friendly	characteristic of or befitting a friend	He always speaks in a friendly way.
Kindhearted	having or proceeding from an innately kind disposition	He is a generous and kindhearted teacher.
Peaceful	not disturbed by strife or turmoil or war	We need a peaceful world.
Steadfast	marked by firm determination or resolution; not shakable	He is steadfast in his faith.
Trustworthy	worthy of trust or belief	He is trustworthy person.

Barack Obama

The Kind, Friendly Man

"A friend is a person with whom I may be sincere. Before him I may think aloud."

– Ralph Waldo Emerson

Barack Obama: The Kind, Friendly Man

```
u n e l b a r e n e v o h r
n c o n g e n i a l i l t i
s i i c t g a m n a v u n d
p i l n i h i u u n a n n e
e i s n c c u s p o c u i s
t l e c a e i s a i i o i o
n b e b g a l n i t o s r p
e a l i e g u u i a u u s m
i e t n a v i p m r s e s o
l o v e o p t i m i s t i c
i m o a u g l a c p n g i t
s u o i t n e i c s n o c c
e b e n e v o l e n t b u n
r e l e t i v l a i n e g s
```

AMICABLE	COMPOSED	ENTHUSIASTIC
LUMINOUS	RESILIENT	BENEVOLENT
CONGENIAL	GENIAL	OPTIMISTIC
VENERABLE	BENIGN	CONSCIENTIOUS
INSPIRATIONAL	PIOUS	VIVACIOUS

(Solution on page 142)

BARACK OBAMA: THE KIND, FRIENDLY MAN

WORD	DEFINITION	SENTENCE
Amicable	characterized by or showing goodwill; friendly;	We prefer to settle disputes through **amicable** conciliation.
Composed	serenely self-possessed and free from agitation especially in times of stress	He appeared **composed** and sensible.
Enthusiastic	having or showing great excitement and interest	I always tell my son to be confident and **enthusiastic**.
Luminous	softly bright or radiant	He is a **luminous** speaker.
Resilient	recovering readily from adversity depression or the like	He is very **resilient** to changes.
Benevolent	intending or showing kindness	We need a **benevolent** society.
Congenial	suitable to your needs or similar to your nature	He found few people **congenial** to him in the party.
Genial	diffusing warmth and friendliness	He is so **genial** that he will make friends wherever he goes.
Optimistic	expecting the best	I'm very **optimistic**.
Venerable	profoundly honored	He is a **venerable** and wise old man.
Benign	pleasant and beneficial in nature or influence	She is a **benign** old lady.
Conscientious	characterized by extreme care and great effort	He is a **conscientious** judge.
Inspirational	under the influence of inspiration	He gave us an **inspirational** speech.
Pious	having or showing or expressing reverence for a deity	They seem to be very **pious**
Vivacious	vigorous and active	She is a **vivacious** and charming hostess.

Barack Obama

The Luminious Man

"The great actors are the luminous ones. They are the great conductors of the stage."

– Ethel Barrymore

Words, Cross & Across

BARACK OBAMA: THE LUMINOUS MAN

```
e s u o r t s u l
t l r d d n e u p
a l l i i a m e d
d i c u l i l c d
i u u c n l c d d
c d e o u l l r l
u e u c c i i i c
l s i l l r u u d
e d u u a b s i m
```

BRILLIANT   LUCID
PELLUCID   ELUCIDATE
LUMINOUS   LUSTROUS

(Solution on page 143)

101

BARACK OBAMA: THE LUMINOUS MAN

WORD	DEFINITION	SENTENCE
Brilliant	of surpassing excellence	We are deeply impressed by his **brilliant** performance.
Lucid	capable of thinking and expressing yourself in a clear and consistent manner	He is a great **lucid** thinker.
Pellucid	easily understandable	He has a **pellucid** mind.
Elucidate	make clear and (more) comprehensible	Please **elucidate** the reasons of your decision.
Luminous	softly bright or radiant	He is a **luminous** speaker.
Lustrous	brilliant	What he did sets a **lustrous** example for others to follow.

102

Barack Obama

*"Life is best enjoyed when
time periods are evenly divided
between labor, sleep, and
rebuilding ... all people should
spend one-third of their time
in recreation which is rebuilding,
voluntary activity, never idleness."*

– Brigham Young

BARACK OBAMA: RECREATION

```
g w r i t i n g l
n r m p o k g p l
i t u o g t i i a
z z s k b z i c b
i e i e g n a u t
n s c r a b b l e
a r n i e b e u k
g n i d a e r s s
r g a a a b e k a
o d r a i l l i b
```

SCRABBLE   POKER   BASKETBALL
READING   MUSIC   BILLIARD
WRITING   ORGANIZING

(Solution on page 144)

BARACK OBAMA: RECREATION

WORD	DEFINITION	SENTENCE
Scrabble	a game of word search	He always seems to have the whip hand over me when we play **scrabble**.
Poker	a card game	He is a man with a **poker** face.
Basketball	a game played on a court by two opposing teams of 5 players	He likes playing **basketball**.
Reading	the cognitive process of understanding a written linguistic message	He enjoys **reading**
Music	an artistic form of auditory communication incorporating instrumental or vocal tones in a structured and continuous manner	**Music** is a kind of universal language.
Billiard	a type of shot in cue sports such as pool, carom billiards and snooker)	He likes playing **billiard**.
Writing	the act of creating written works	**Writing** was a form of therapy for him.
Organizing	cause to be structured or ordered or operating according to some principle or idea	He is leader with excellent **organizing** ability.

Barack Obama

The Intelligent Man

*"The trouble with the world
is that the stupid
are cocksure and
the intelligent
are full of doubt."*

– Bertrand Russell

BARACK OBAMA: THE INTELLIGENT MAN

```
r a l o h c s g i a t t v s
e o w h a r v a r d a a s l o
r o t a n e s i r e p r s e n
t r e i e n s l s a h e u c y
i n c i d t r o t i o z o t w
u r e i n e e q v i o i i u n
e l p d y r v u y i i n c r u
t t t w u p i a m c u a a e w
i d a c c r t c v m l g g r o
p l v r e i p i m e a r a i y
t i e d y s e o l r a o s e s
u h a r t i c u l a t e c s n
p e g e c n r s r o h t u a o
r d l i n g e n i o u s e r t
u w i e r e p c o r v c i e i
a c o t h b r o v g a o o u t
```

ARTICULATE AUTHOR BRIGHT
COMMUNITY EDITOR ENTERPRISING
HARVARD INGENIOUS LAWYER
LECTURER LOQUACIOUS ORGANIZER
PERCEPTIVE PRUDENT READER
SAGACIOUS SCHOLAR SENATOR
VISIONARY

(Solution on page 145)

BARACK OBAMA: THE INTELLIGENT MAN

WORD	DEFINITION	SENTENCE
Articulate	expressing yourself easily or characterized by clear expressive language	He is the most **articulate** among the children.
Author	person who write a novel, poem, essay, etc.	I finally met the famous **author** of Harry potter.
Bright	having striking color	**Bright** colours attract babies.
Community	a group of people living in a particular local area	The **community** needs more volunteers.
Editor	a person responsible for the editorial aspects of publication; the person who determines the final content of a text especially of a newspaper or magazine)	He became the chief **editor** in his early thirties.
Enterprising	marked by aggressive ambition and energy and initiative	He is an **enterprising** young man.
Harvard	a famous university in Massachusetts	**Harvard** university is one of the best universities in the world.
Ingenious	used of persons or artifacts) marked by independence and creativity in thought or action	Your invention is **ingenious**, but not very practical.
Lawyer	a professional person authorized to practice law; conducts lawsuits or gives legal advice	He is a notable **lawyer**.
Lecturer	someone who lectures professionally	The **lecturer** kindled my interest.
Loquacious	talking or tending to talk much or freely	**Loquacious** neighbors are always annoying.

Barack
Obama

A Sociable Man

*"Be civil to all,
sociable to many,
familiar with few,
friend to one,
enemy to none."*

– Franz Kafka

BARACK OBAMA: A SOCIABLE MAN

```
e x t r o v e r t e d a
l s b o e e g c e g a r
b l e m g t u e d r g a
a e v g g a c o c e x t
n l t v r r m o t g t c
o a e a e e i a g i g t
i i f v g e g e e o o o
n v n e a b a t u a g
a i e a r c r e t s l o
p v v g i v g g g e p d
m n n e o t e e g e n o
o o a t u s v n g a r u
c c e g s i e r t g v n
```

AGGREGATE   COMPANIONABLE
CONGREGATE   CONVIVIAL
EGREGIOUS   EXTROVERTED
FERVENT   GREGARIOUS
SEGREGATE

(Solution on page 146)

BARACK OBAMA: A SOCIABLE MAN

WORD	DEFINITION	SENTENCE
Aggregate	gather in a mass, sum, or whole	The money donated will **aggregate** a thousand dollars.
Companionable	having the good qualities of a companion; associating with the other	Pandas are **companionable** animals.
Congregate	come together, usually for a purpose	People quickly **congregated** round the speaker.
Convivial	occupied with or fond of the pleasures of good company	She is a **convivial** woman.
Egregious	conspicuously and outrageously bad or reprehensible	She made an **egregious** mistake.
Extraverted	being concerned with the social and physical environment	She is an **extraverted** girl.
Fervent	characterized by intense emotion	He has a **fervent** desire to change the society.
Gregarious	seeking and enjoying the company of others	Human beings are **gregarious**.
Segregate	separate or isolate one thing) from another and place in a group apart from others;	The doctor **segregated** the child sick with scarlet fever.

114

Barack
Obama

A Physical Man

*Knowledge of every aspect
of human life, physical and
spiritual is plentiful today.*

BARACK OBAMA: A PHYSICAL MAN

```
e p s c d h r l s o i a
c s v w e s s s ml t n
i l a w r i h d r s n e
o p i t r e p p a d n v
v c a h s o c e e a mo
e h t i l l c y mt t y
n t k n i i e k o d a b
o r d t m - e n s r o o
t e i a n h i s d t l k
i r b w e b v l n e a t
r h o e l r l l a p r r
a r k a p a b n h r r n
b r e p c e e o d i e d
```

BROWN-EYED	HANDSOME
LEAN	DAPPER
BARITONE VOICE	ROCK STAR
LITHE	SLENDER
SLIM	THIN

(Solution on page 147)

117

BARACK OBAMA: A PHYSICAL MAN

WORD	DEFINITION	SENTENCE
Brown eyed	person with eyes in the color of brown	He is a **brown eyed** young man.
Handsome	pleasing in appearance especially by reason of conformity to ideals of form and proportion	He is a **handsome** young man.
Lean	lacking excess flesh	He has a **lean** and sinewy frame.
Dapper	marked by smartness in dress and manners	He is a **dapper** young man.
Baritone voice	lower in range than tenor and higher than bass	He has a charming **baritone voice**.
Rock star	a famous singer of rock music	The **rock star** overdosed and was found dead in his hotel room.
Lithe	gracefully slender; moving and bending with ease	She is a **lithe** ballet dancer.
Slender	being of delicate	His body is **slender**.
Slim	being of delicate or slender build	She is a **slim** girl with straight blonde hair.
Thin	of relatively small extent from one surface to the opposite or in cross section	He is **thin** in the face.

SOLUTIONS

Words

Cross & Across

Word Search on Barack Obama

THE OBAMAS: A FRIENDLY FAMILY

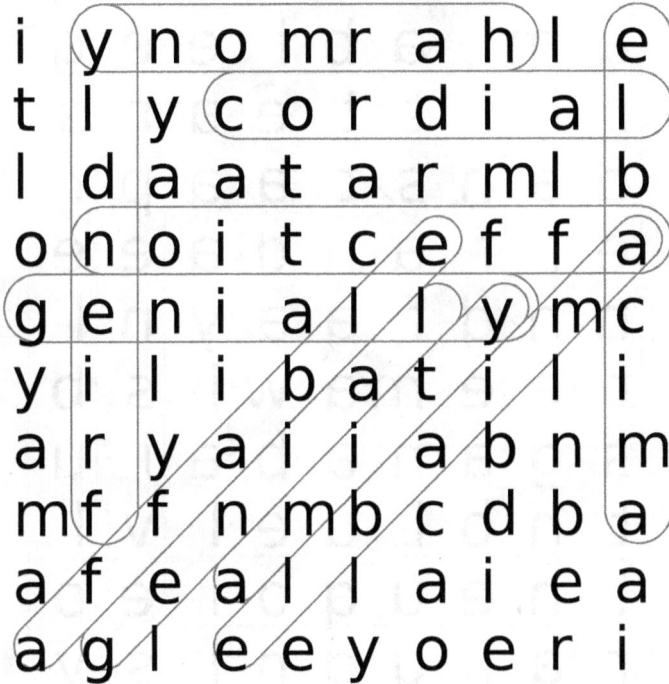

```
i  y  n  o  m  r  a  h  l  e
t  l  y  c  o  r  d  i  a  l
l  d  a  a  t  a  r  m  l  b
o  n  o  i  t  c  e  f  f  a
g  e  n  i  a  l  l  y  m  c
y  i  l  i  b  a  t  i  l  i
a  r  y  a  i  i  a  b  n  m
m  f  f  n  m  b  c  d  b  a
a  f  e  a  l  l  a  i  e  a
a  g  l  e  e  y  o  e  r  i
```

AFFABLE   AFFECTION   AMIABLE
AMICABLE   AMITY   FRIENDLY
GENIAL   GENIALLY   CORDIAL
HARMONY

BARACK'S WIFE: MICHELLE OBAMA

```
a m i   a b l   e   g
r l   l t t e a r s
d a n s t a a p r
e i f a n d a e e
n n d f a a y n l
t e e m a w i s b
s g a n a b a i u
t n b l u e l v l
t n e u q o l e o
r a l u g n i s v
```

ARDENT   ELOQUENT   AFFABLE
LAWYER   GENIAL   ADAMANT
SEDATE   PENSIVE   SINGULAR
VOLUBLE   AMIABLE

BARACK'S OLDER DAUGHTER: MALIA OBAMA

```
e  t  c  u  r  i  o  u  s  h
v  h  e  u  i  v  o  d  b  a
i  o  a  l  r  i  u  c  i  m
t  u  c  b  b  v  u  e  o  i
c  g  e  l  b  a  r  o  d  a
a  h  m  i  t  c  c  b  u  f
a  t  e  v  u  i  i  i  a  a
r  f  h  p  h  o  t  f  m  t
l  u  f  i  t  u  a  e  b  a
u  l  p  o  i  s  e  d  v  u
```

ACTIVE	CURIOUS
BEAUTIFUL	ADORABLE
POISED	THOUGHTFUL
VIVACIOUS	AMICABLE

BARACK'S YOUNGER DAUGHTER: SASHA OBAMA

```
c u r i o u s d r l s
d q e l b a r o d a p
e i e u e e d m h d o
r i f f d e s i o p l
e v i t i s i u q n i
a y f h a l e r t o t
d p e g n b i t r l e
e p r u t o i k o c n
r a m o r o u s i p b
s h d h s a i n u n n
l i i t a e m e p e d
```

INQUISITIVE   AMOROUS   ADORABLE
NICE   KIND   POISED
ALERT   HAPPY   CURIOUS
POLITE   THOUGHTFUL   OBEDIENT
READER

Barack's Mother: Ann Dunham

```
a c f r q r q e f k r a d l r
n p i a p q e r w e q r e a e
v b x t u z i h h m h w n e s
p b m y s e r c t z o t i n o
u h q l n i r e a o h c m j l
r f b d d a l k t r m c r f u
c k l j e a z a o w b c e n t
g y b s t w e p e w u c t h e
d j e p n a o s z d t f e d t
n r z g h l c o r a i n d j e
b t u i o p t i m i s t i c i
t e n g i l l e t n i y y d u
t r i f j l q e z u e u x n q
w s r e m a e r d l r h t g h
t w q v y w d b g j n n n i y
```

MOTHER   **QUIET**
TACITURN   **RESEARCHER**
INTELLIGENT   **OPTIMISTIC**
DREAMER   **RESOLUTE**
IDEALISTIC   **ANTHROPOLGIST**
DETERMINED   **FRIENDLY**

BARACK'S MATERNAL GRANDMOTHER:
MADELYN DUNHAM

```
e a g e e t b t t t r f
c t r n m p r n d n p n
t n a h i r s e t s r c
e n n n h r o e a a o t
e r d t o r a r t m t e
e m m h e i t c p f e t
v s o h l u s e i l c m
y h t r o w t s u r t o
n o h r b e c t a o i m
m w e g n a s e s p v r
g t r t l s n g i n e b
a e a i v g e k e i p t
```

CARING   COMPETENT
FISCAL   BANK
MOTHER   PASSIONATE
PROTECTIVE   TRUSTWORTHY
GRANDMOTHER   BENIGN

BARACK'S MATERNAL GRANDFATHER:
STANLEY DUNHAM

```
u  y  t  n  a  i  l  a  v  a  m
s  l  d  g  a  f  a  t  h  e  r
h  d  c  t  n  m  y  u  e  d  f
t  n  e  i  l  i  s  e  r  a  l
h  e  g  s  t  b  m  e  n  y  e
e  i  d  c  a  e  g  r  l  c  m
l  r  a  n  s  e  g  l  a  a  e
p  f  d  e  n  c  c  r  n  h  s
f  r  p  l  a  c  i  e  e  r  c
u  e  e  a  i  n  r  e  d  n  c
l  d  n  i  g  t  a  e  r  e  e
```

RESILIENT	HUSBAND	VALIANT
FATHER	FRIENDLY	CARING
DECEASED	CHARMING	HELPFUL
ENERGETIC	SALESMAN	

BARACK OBAMA: THE ORATOR

```
r i e o e e o r i e e k
r h a r l e b e p c p h
s p e a k e r k s l p s
h s k t e k e a p e e i
e r k i o a i e i r n a
p p m o s r f p h r k h
r f i n a i i s e e m k
s r e k a m h c e e p s
s a h p k s c i i i r b
e r e a a s e l c a i r
s n c r i e e b r e n s
o h e s h e p u a k r b
r s s n t n s p e e c h
```

SPEAKER

SPEECH

RHETORICIAN

SPEECHIFIER

ORATION

PUBLIC SPEAKER

SPEECHMAKER

BARACK OBAMA: THE AUDACIOUS MAN

```
b a a c s n n n b a e o
e o s l b m d d n r a n
s h l b r a s h n e s s
r a c d a c y i n c b d
g d e i v a r d d n r a
y t i r e m e t i e a r
y p n e f b t d p d s i
a s s u r a n c e i h n
s s e n d l o b r f n g
g e m o s e r u t n e v
v e o r y c f n n o s i
c l r n s s f r i c s t
d a u n t l e s s d n n
```

BOLD
ASSURANCE
GALL
BRAVE
BRASHNESS
DARING
DAUNTLESS

TEMERITY
BRASHNESS
EFFRONTERY
CONFIDENCE
BOLDNESS
VENTURESOME
INTREPID

BARACK OBAMA: THE INTELLECTUAL

```
g n i e i d l s a i e u
n o a e r d e i m e r a
i s t e s i s n u a a n
d a i t s e i n i a r b
n e d u c a t e d a a t
a r t n n e n n c e r a
t n e g i l l e t n i b
s d l i u m t l t t a r
r l e c n t c n e i e a
e c n e g i l l e t n i
d s c h o l a r s n n n
n i c e r e b r a l l i
u m t n e i b e b m u g
```

INTELLIGENT	SMART
REASON	UNDERSTANDING
INTELLECT	BRAIN
INTELLIGENCE	BRAINED
MIND	BRAINIER
BRAINIEST	EDUCATED
SCHOLAR	CEREBRAL

Barack Obama: The Powerful Man

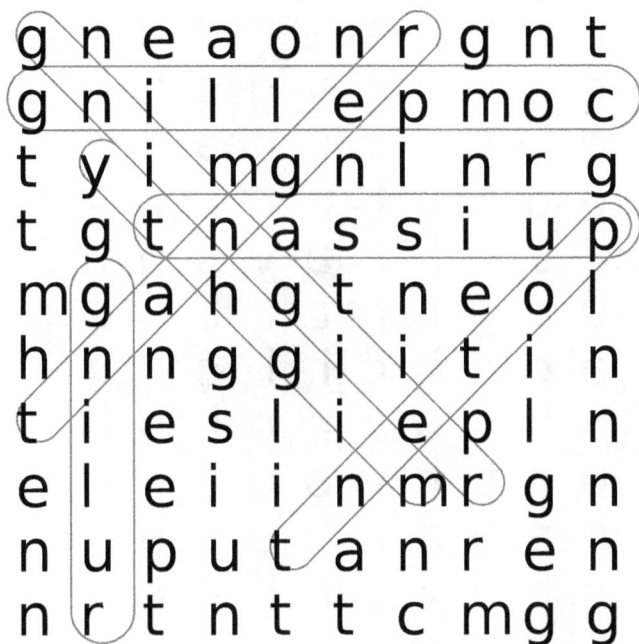

```
g n e a o n r g n t
g n i l l e p m o c
t y i m g n l n r g
t g t n a s s i u p
m g a h g t n e o l
h n n g g i i t i n
t i e s l i e p l n
e l e i i n m r g n
n u p u t a n r e n
n r t n t t c m g g
```

MIGHTY   RULING

REIGNING   COMPELLING

POTENT   REGNANT

PUISSANT

Barack Obama: The Decisive Man

```
e t u l o s e r o u t f
v t i i v f v g s a l i
i e i t s p i r a u r u
t u o t o l t m i f v t
a i t t l i a v p n u f
c u p g t m t i t o i i
i a c c i c i l c i r f
f o t i a s r r i u i t
i u r t r v o u f l r v
n i a o a r h e r u i c
g i t n v g t i r c i o
i i i t a e u s t l i i
s a s u e n a i i t v o
```

RESOLUTE

OF IMPORT

AUTHORITATIVE

CRUCIAL

SIGNIFICATIVE

Words, Cross & Across

BARACK OBAMA: A MAN EMBRACING CHANGE

```
n l x c s q a y g o d y l g n
a o q y w o l j s y f h h q l
k c i n o i t a c i f i d o m
s n t t l q e f d o x u o g z
l d e i a i r o b n o c n g l
l p y u o r m r e v i s e g y
s n f b h n e n m i r g w s f
r o x a y r q t a y a n o v d
h i f f c m x t l z n u f o c
n s y y n s i w m a r z w i g
m i v x c f a n e r x i j l t
p v m l x x m e x o u m j m h
h e j g x z b f b n m d d g p
w r z w r l b g u j p e v a x
w h l h s w n x r x a x l g e
```

ALTERATION   **ACTION**
MODIFY   **ALTER**
MODIFICATION   **REVISION**
REVISE

133

BARACK OBAMA: A MAN OF FAITH

```
s c t g a e c a c l a
s n o e c s a e a e r
e s o m l a i t c i n
n t i i m e t n a i o
l s a t g i a y i b i
u c o m m i t m e n t
f a f m g i l l m r a
h n o e l c i e u a c
t c l e c e o s r f i
i l d b f b t t n t d
a i a l a l f f e t e
f t l l i r e a i i d
```

TRUST

BELIEF

RELIGION

FAITHFULNESS

FIDELITY

ALLEGIANCE

COMMITMENT

DEDICATION

COMMITTAL

COMMIT

BARACK OBAMA: THE DETERMINED MAN

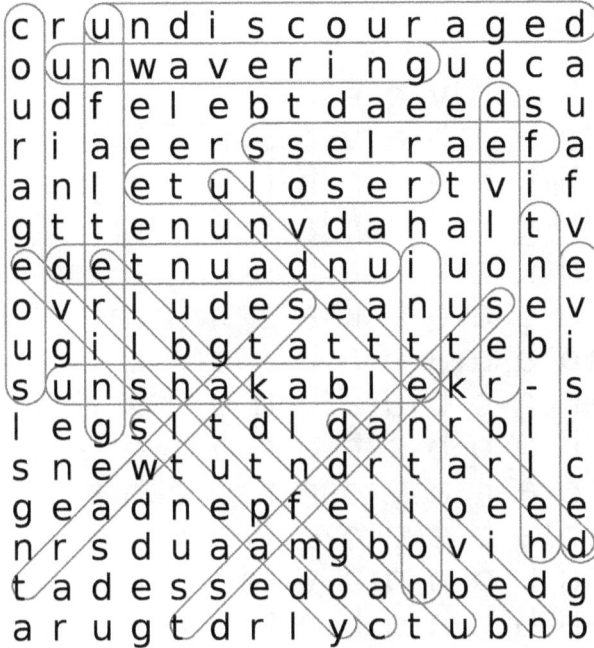

```
c r u n d i s c o u r a g e d
o u n w a v e r i n g u d c a
u d f e l e b t d a e e d s u
r i a e e r s s e l r a e f a
a n l e t u l o s e r t v i f
g t t e n u n v d a h a l t v
e d e t n u a d n u i u o n e
o v r l u d e s e a n u s e v
u g i l b g t a t t t t e b i
s u n s h a k a b l e k r - s
l e g s t d l d a n r b l i
s n e w t u t n d r t a r l c
g e a d n e p f e l i o e e e
n r s d u a a m g b o v i h d
t a d e s s e d o a n b e d g
a r u g t d r l y c t u b n b
```

RESOLUTE
COMPULSIVE
DECISIVE
UNFALTERING
UNWAVERING
STALWART
UNDETERRED
INTENTION
UNBENDABLE
FEARLESS

DRIVEN
COURAGEOUS
UNSHAKABLE
HELL-BENT
RESOLVED
UNDAUNTED
UNDISCOURAGED
STEADFAST
STEADY

Barack Obama: The Loquacious Man

```
d l e h y g e a e d e e e
e e a i h a v b e l y t a
h h i t a r i h g t o b y
t t g l c r t a l k y i r
u d k m k u a t u l c a t
o g g d o l k a s h u m h
m o a m a o l b a g r g m
r r g b t u a t u u d s i
e i u b b s t g e a r e b
b b a r a y o m r t e b v
b b a b e g o s y a c a u
a u l g b m a v m a u u t
l b b l h e l a l b h y a
b u a b d r g t h r g l a
```

CHATTY

GARRULOUS

TALKATIVE

BIGMOUTHED

GABBY

TALKY

BLABBER MOUTHED

BARACK OBAMA: THE PEACE MAKER

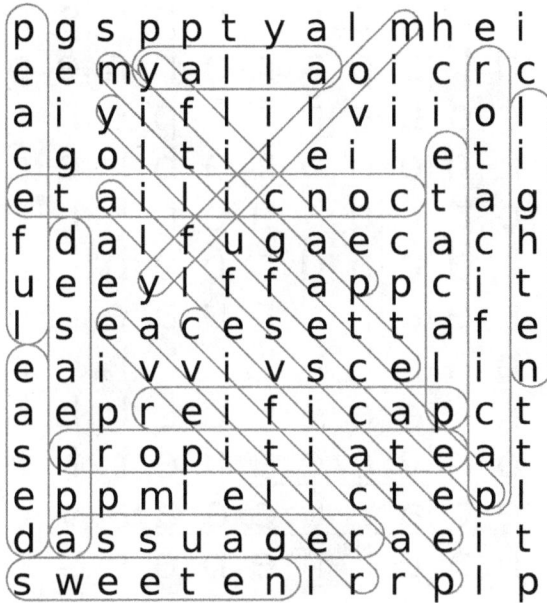

```
p g s p p t y a l m h e i
e e m y a l l a o i c r c
a i y i f l i l v i i o l
c g o l t i l e i l e t i
e t a i l i c n o c t a g
f d a l f u g a e c a c h
u e e y l f f a p p c i t
l s e a c e s e t t a f e
e a i v v i v s c e l i n
a e p r e i f i c a p c t
s p r o p i t i a t e a t
e p p m l e l i c t e p l
d a s s u a g e r a e i t
s w e e t e n l r r p l p
```

PEACEFUL   PEACEFULLY   PACIFICATOR
PACIFY   MOLLIFY   PACIFIER
PACIFIC   APPEASED   ASSUAGER
PLACATE   SWEETEN   CONCILIATE
PROPITIATE   RELIEVE   ALLAY
EASED   MITIGATE   LIGHTEN
ALLEVIATE

Barack Obama: An Honest Man

```
d o o d r e h r d s u p c
n n a e r e c n i s n s h
d l s p s r d r n e p b s
c o u e r s f p b l r i e
r h o n o r a b l e e u a
o t i d t u o r l l t u u
t d c a d r u e b i e a s
t e a b t r u a e u n l a
b a r l i t i t r g t o n
r f e e e l u t h b i l g
o h v c e a u e t f o l u
e t a r u c c a a v u r p
n a e i r e b e e s s l a
```

UNPRETENTIOUS   UNTRUTHFUL
VERACIOUS   HONORABLE
RELIABLE   DEPENDABLE
GUILELESS   SINCERE
TRUE   ACCURATE

BARACK OBAMA: THE RESOURCEFUL MAN

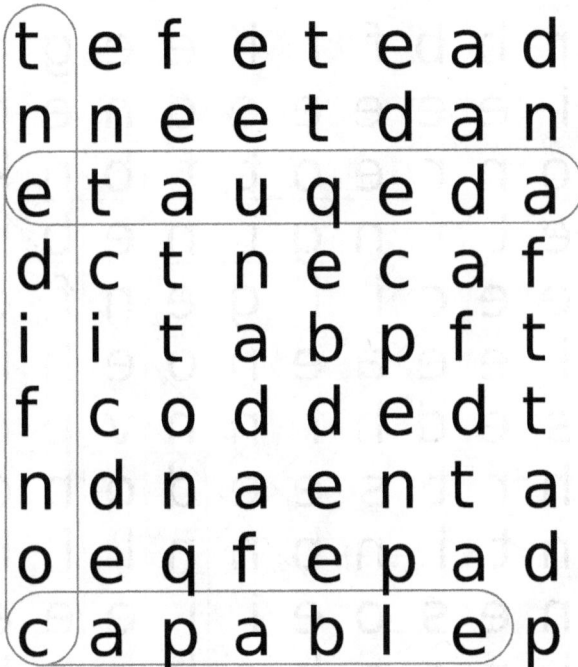

```
t e f e t e a d
n n e e t d a n
e t a u q e d a
d c t n e c a f
i i t a b p f t
f c o d d e d t
n d n a e n t a
o e q f e p a d
c a p a b l e p
```

CAPABLE   CONFIDENT
ADEQUATE

BARACK OBAMA:
MAKING THINGS GO WELL AND BEING KIND

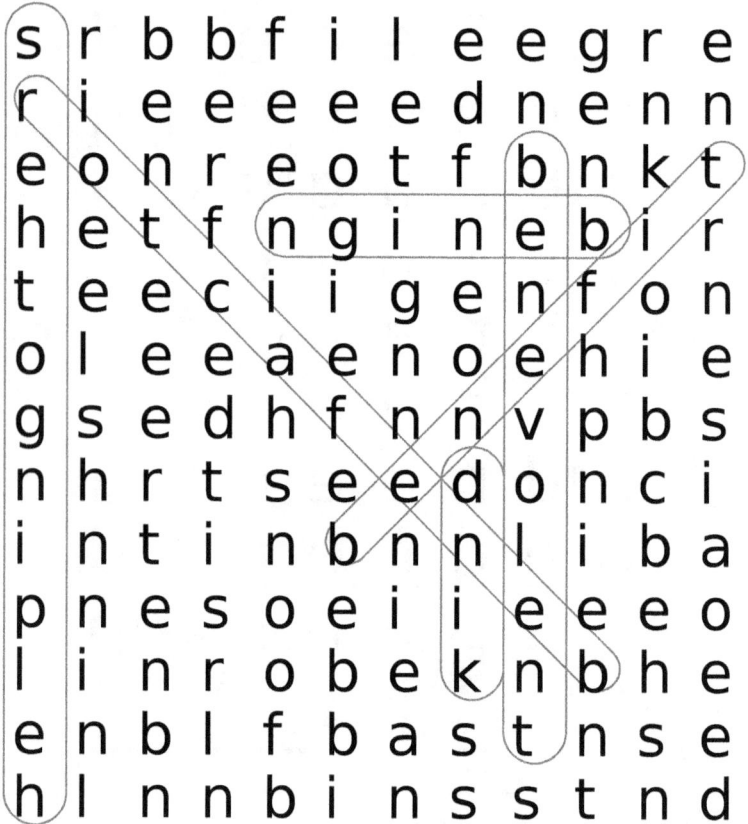

```
s r b b f i l e e g r e
r i e e e e e d n e n n
e o n r e o t f b n k t
h e t f n g i n e b i r
t e e c i i g e n f o n
o l e e a e n o e h i e
g s e d h f n v p b s
n h r t s e e d o n c i
i n t i n b n n l i b a
p n e s o e i i e e e o
l i n r o b e k n b h e
e n b l f b a s t n s e
h l n n b i n s s t n d
```

BENEFACTOR   BENIGN
BENEFIT   HELPING OTHERS
BENEVOLENT   KIND

BARACK OBAMA: THE POSITIVE FORCE

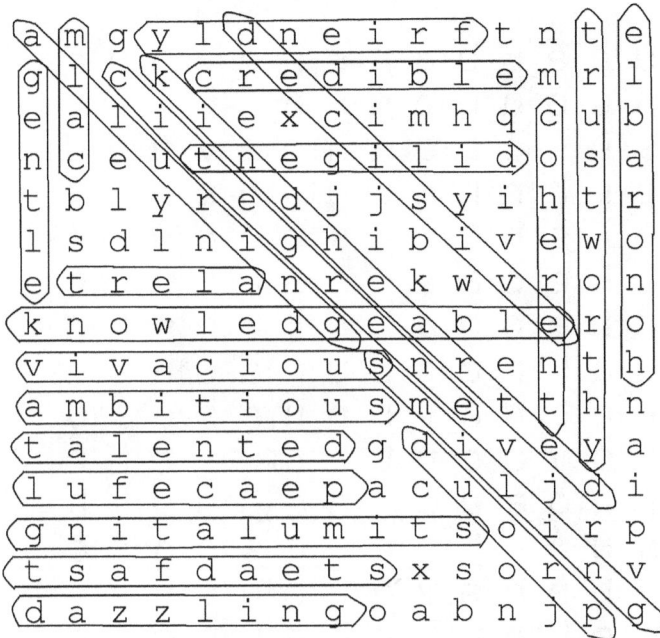

```
a m g y l d n e i r f t n t e
g l c k c r e d i b l e m r l
e a l i i e x c i m h q c u b
n c e u t n e g i l i d o s a
t b l y r e d j j s y i h t r
l s d l n i g h i b i v e w o
e t r e l a n r e k w v r o n
k n o w l e d g e a b l e r o
v i v a c i o u s n r e n t h
a m b i t i o u s m e t t h n
t a l e n t e d g d i v e y a
l u f e c a e p a c u l j d i
g n i t a l u m i t s o i r p
t s a f d a e t s x s o r n v
d a z z l i n g o a b n j p g
```

AMBITIOUS	DILIGENT	FRIENDLY
ENERGETIC	CALM	COHERENT
CREDIBLE	ALERT	ALLURING
DAZZLING	DECISIVE	PROUD
SMILING	STEADFAST	GENTLE
HONORABLE	KINDHEARTED	KNOWLEDGEABLE
PEACEFUL	STIMULATING	TALENTED
TRUSTWORTHY	VIVACIOUS	

141

BARACK OBAMA: THE KIND, FRIENDLY MAN

```
u n e l b a r e n e v o h r
n c o n g e n i a l i l t i
s i i c t g a m n a v u n d
p i l n i h i u u n a n n e
e i s n c c u s p o c u i s
t l e c a e i s a i i o i o
n b e b g a n i t o s r p
e a l i e g u u i a u u s m
i e t n a v i p m r s e s o
l o v e o p t i m i s t i c
i m o a u g l a c p n g i t
s u o i t n e i c s n o c c
e b e n e v o l e n t b u n
r e l e t i v l a i n e g s
```

AMICABLE	COMPOSED	ENTHUSIASTIC
LUMINOUS	RESILIENT	BENEVOLENT
CONGENIAL	GENIAL	OPTIMISTIC
VENERABLE	BENIGN	CONSCIENTIOUS
INSPIRATIONAL	PIOUS	VIVACIOUS

BARACK OBAMA: THE LUMINOUS MAN

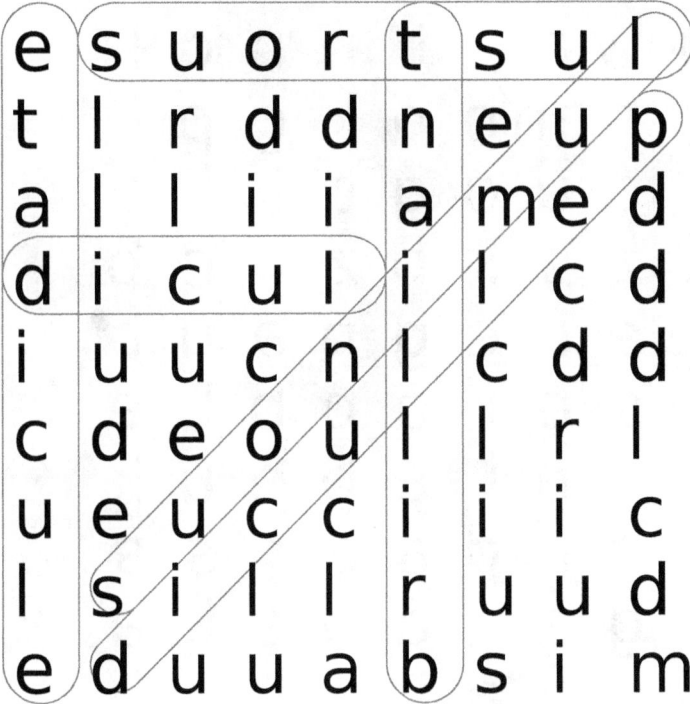

```
e s u o r t s u l
t l r d d n e u p
a l l i i a m e d
d i c u l i l c d
i u u c n l c d d
c d e o u l r l
u e u c c i i i c
l s i l l r u u d
e d u u a b s i m
```

BRILLIANT   **LUCID**
PELLUCID   **ELUCIDATE**
LUMINOUS   **LUSTROUS**

BARACK OBAMA: RECREATION

```
g w r i t i n g l
n r m p o k g p l
i t u o g t i i a
z z s k b z i c b
i e i e g n a u t
n s c r a b b l e
a r n i e b e u k
g n i d a e r s s
r g a a a b e k a
o d r a i l l i b
```

SCRABBLE   POKER   BASKETBALL
READING   MUSIC   BILLIARD
WRITING   ORGANIZING

BARACK OBAMA: THE INTELLIGENT MAN

```
r a l o h c s g i a t t v s
e o w h a r v a r d a a s l o
r o t a n e s i r e p r s e n
t r e i e n s l s a h e u c y
i n c i d t r o t i o z o t w
u r e i n e e q v i o i i u n
e l p d y r v u y i i n c r u
t t t w u p i a m c u a a e w
i d a c c r t c v m l g g r o
p l v r e i p i m e a r a i y
t i e d y s e o l r a o s e s
u h a r t i c u l a t e c s n
p e g e c n r s r o h t u a o
r d l i n g e n i o u s e r t
u w i e r e p c o r v c i e i
a c o t h b r o v g a o o u t
```

ARTICULATE   AUTHOR   BRIGHT
COMMUNITY   EDITOR   ENTERPRISING
HARVARD   INGENIOUS   LAWYER
LECTURER   LOQUACIOUS   ORGANIZER
PERCEPTIVE   PRUDENT   READER
SAGACIOUS   SCHOLAR   SENATOR
VISIONARY

Words, Cross & Across

BARACK OBAMA: A SOCIABLE MAN

```
e x t r o v e r t e d a
l s b o e e g c e g a r
b l e m g t u e d r g a
a e v g g a c o c e x t
n l t v r r m o t g t c
o a e a e e i a g i g t
i i f v g e g e e o o o
n v n e a e b a t u a g
a i e a r c r e t s l o
p v v g i v g g g e p d
m n n e o t e e g e n o
o o a t u s v n g a r u
c c e g s i e r t g v n
```

AGGREGATE   COMPANIONABLE
CONGREGATE   CONVIVIAL
EGREGIOUS   EXTROVERTED
FERVENT   GREGARIOUS
SEGREGATE

146

Barack Obama: A Physical Man

```
e p s c d h r l s o i a
c s v w e s s s m l t n
i l a w r i h d r s n e
o p i t r e p p a d n v
v c a h s o c e e a m o
e h t i l l c y m t t y
n t k n i i e k o d a b
o r d t m - e n s r o o
t e i a n h i s d t l k
i r b w e b v l n e a t
r h o e l r l l a p r r
a r k a p a b n h r r n
b r e p c e e o d i e d
```

BROWN-EYED   HANDSOME
LEAN   DAPPER
BARITONE VOICE   ROCK STAR
LITHE   SLENDER
SLIM   THIN

Sources for This Book:

Magazines

- Time Magazine   May 19,2008 "How He Learned To Win" Michael Weisskopt
- Time Magazine   April 21, 2008 "A Mother's Story" Amanda Ripley
- Jet Magazine   May 26,2008   "History In The Making" Kevin Chappell
- Esquire Magazine June 2008 "Get Ready To Rumble" Richard Walter

Books

- "Barack Obama: In His Own Words" Lisa Rogak
- "Obama: From Promise To Power" David Mendell
- "Dreams From My Father" Barack Obama

CD's

- "Dreams From My Father" Barack Obama

Speech by Barack Obama on being elected the 44th President of the United States of America

Chicago, November 4, 2008

Hello, Chicago. If there is anyone out there who still doubts that America is a place where all things are possible, who still wonders if the dream of our founders is alive in our time, who still questions the power of our democracy, tonight is your answer.

It's the answer told by lines that stretched around schools and churches in numbers this nation has never seen, by people who waited three hours and four hours, many for the first time in their lives, because they believed that this time must be different, that their voices could be that difference.

It's the answer spoken by young and old, rich and poor, Democrat and Republican, black, white, Hispanic, Asian, Native American, gay, straight, disabled and not disabled. Americans who sent a message to the world that we have never been just a collection of individuals or a collection of red states and blue states. We are, and always will be, the United States of America.

It's the answer that led those who've been told for so long by so many to be cynical and fearful and doubtful about what we can achieve to put their hands on the arc of history and bend it once more toward the hope of a better day.

It's been a long time coming, but tonight, because of what we did on this date in this election at this defining moment change has come to America.

A little bit earlier this evening, I received an extraordinarily gracious call from Senator McCain. Senator McCain fought long and hard in this campaign. And he's fought even longer and harder for the country that he loves. He has endured sacrifices for America that most of us cannot begin to imagine. We are better off for the service rendered by this brave and selfless leader.

I congratulate him; I congratulate Governor Palin for all that they've achieved. And I look forward to working with them to renew this nation's promise in the months ahead.

I want to thank my partner in this journey, a man who campaigned from his heart, and spoke for the men and women he grew up with on the streets of Scranton ... and rode with on the train home to Delaware, the vice president-elect of the United States, Joe Biden.

And I would not be standing here tonight without the unyielding support of my best friend for the last 16 years ... the rock of our family, the love of my life, the nation's next first lady ... Michelle Obama. Sasha and Malia ... I love you both more than you can imagine. And you have earned the new puppy that's coming with us ...to the new White House.

And while she's no longer with us, I know my grandmother's watching, along with the family that made me who I am. I miss them tonight. I know that my debt to them is beyond measure.

To my sister Maya, my sister Alma, all my other brothers and sisters, thank you so much for all the support that you've given me. I am grateful to them.

And to my campaign manager, David Plouffe ... the unsung hero of this campaign, who built the best–the best political campaign, I think, in the history of the United States of America.

To my chief strategist David Axelrod ... who's been a partner with me every step of the way. To the best campaign team ever assembled in the history of politics ... you made this happen, and I am forever grateful for what you've sacrificed to get it done.

But above all, I will never forget who this victory truly belongs to. It belongs to you. It belongs to you.

I was never the likeliest candidate for this office. We didn't start with much money or many endorsements. Our campaign was not hatched in the halls of Washington. It began in the backyards of Des Moines and the living rooms of Concord and the front porches of Charleston.

It was built by working men and women who dug into what little savings they had to give $5 and $10 and $20 to the cause. It grew strength from the young people who rejected the myth of their generation's apathy ... who left their homes and their families for jobs that offered little pay and less sleep; from the not-so-young people who braved the bitter cold and scorching heat to knock on the doors of perfect strangers; from the millions of Americans who volunteered, and organized, and proved that more than two centuries later, a government of the people, by the people and for the people has not perished from this Earth. This is your victory.

I know you didn't do this just to win an election and I know you didn't do it for me. You did it because you understand the enormity of the task that lies ahead. For even as we celebrate tonight, we know the challenges that tomorrow will bring are the greatest of our lifetime, two wars, a planet in peril, the worst financial crisis in a century.

Even as we stand here tonight, we know there are brave Americans waking up in the deserts of Iraq and the mountains of Afghanistan to risk their lives for us. There are mothers and fathers who will lie awake after their children fall asleep and wonder how they'll make the mortgage, or pay their doctor's bills, or save enough for college. There is new energy to harness and new jobs to be created; new schools to build and threats to meet and alliances to repair.

The road ahead will be long. Our climb will be steep. We may not get there in one year or even in one term. But, America, I have never been more hopeful than I am tonight that we will get there. I promise you, we as a people will get there.

There will be setbacks and false starts. There are many who won't agree with every decision or policy I make as president. And we know the government can't solve every problem. But I will always be honest with you about the challenges we face. I will listen to you, especially when we disagree. And, above all, I will ask you to join in the work of remaking this nation, the only way it's been done in America for 221 years—block by block, brick by brick, calloused hand by calloused hand.

What began 21 months ago in the depths of winter cannot end on this autumn night. This victory alone is not the change we seek. It is only the chance for us to make that change. And that cannot happen if we go back to the way things were. It can't happen without you, without a new spirit of service, a new spirit of sacrifice.

So let us summon a new spirit of patriotism, of responsibility, where each of us resolves to pitch in and work harder and look after not only ourselves but each other.

Let us remember that, if this financial crisis taught us anything, it's that we cannot have a thriving Wall Street while Main Street suffers. In this country, we rise or fall as one nation, as one people. Let's resist the temptation to fall back on the same partisanship and pettiness and immaturity that has poisoned our politics for so long.

Let's remember that it was a man from this state who first carried the banner of the Republican Party to the White House, a party founded on the values of self-reliance and individual liberty and national unity. Those are values that we all share. And while the Democratic Party has won a great victory tonight, we do so with a measure of humility and determination to heal the divides that have held back our progress.

As Lincoln said to a nation far more divided than ours, we are not enemies but friends. Though passion may have strained, it must not break our bonds of affection.

And to those Americans whose support I have yet to earn, I may not have won your vote tonight, but I hear your voices. I need your help. And I will be your president, too.

And to all those watching tonight from beyond our shores, from parliaments and palaces, to those who are huddled around radios in the forgotten corners of the world, our stories are singular, but our destiny is shared, and a new dawn of American leadership is at hand.

To those who would tear the world down: We will defeat you. To those who seek peace and security: We support you. And to all those who have wondered if America's beacon still burns as bright: Tonight we proved once more that the true strength of our nation comes not from the might of our arms or the scale of our wealth, but from the enduring power of our ideals: democracy, liberty, opportunity and unyielding hope.

For that's the true genius of America: that America can change. Our union can be perfected. What we've already achieved gives us hope for what we can and must achieve tomorrow.

This election had many firsts and many stories that will be told for generations. But one that's on my mind tonight's about a woman who cast her ballot in Atlanta. She's a lot like the millions of others who stood in line to make their voice heard in this election except for one thing: Ann Nixon Cooper is 106 years old.

She was born just a generation past slavery; a time when there were no cars on the road or planes in the sky; when someone like her couldn't vote for two reasons—because she was a woman and because of the color of her skin.

And tonight, I think about all that she's seen throughout her century in America—the heartache and the hope; the struggle and the progress; the times we were told that we can't, and the people who pressed on with that American creed: Yes we can.

At a time when women's voices were silenced and their hopes dismissed, she lived to see them stand up and speak out and reach for the ballot. Yes we can.

When there was despair in the dust bowl and depression across the land, she saw a nation conquer fear itself with a New Deal, new jobs, a new sense of common purpose. Yes we can.

When the bombs fell on our harbor and tyranny threatened the world, she was there to witness a generation rise to greatness and a democracy was saved. Yes we can.

She was there for the buses in Montgomery, the hoses in Birmingham, a bridge in Selma, and a preacher from Atlanta who told a people that We Shall Overcome. Yes we can.

A man touched down on the moon, a wall came down in Berlin, a world was connected by our own science and imagination. And this year, in this election, she touched her finger to a screen, and cast her vote, because after 106 years in America, through the best of times and the darkest of hours, she knows how America can change. Yes we can.

America, we have come so far. We have seen so much. But there is so much more to do. So tonight, let us ask ourselves—if our children should live to see the next century; if my daughters should be so lucky to live as long as Ann Nixon Cooper, what change will they see? What progress will we have made?

This is our chance to answer that call. This is our moment. This is our time, to put our people back to work and open doors of opportunity for our kids; to restore prosperity and promote the cause of peace; to reclaim the American dream and reaffirm that fundamental truth, that, out of many, we are one; that while we breathe, we hope. And where we are met with cynicism and doubts and those who tell us that we can't, we will respond with that timeless creed that sums up the spirit of a people: Yes, we can.

Thank you. God bless you. And may God bless the United States of America.

Dr. Eugene Williams, Sr.

DR. EUGENE WILLIAMS, SR. is a well-known public school and college teacher, author researcher rand administrator. As the Director of Academic Enhancement in the Washington, D.C. Public Schools, Dr. Williams implemented a highly effective test improvement program which dramatically increased the number of National Merit, National Achievement, and Hispanic scholars in D.C. Schools.

He is a prolific writer and has spoken at several national conventions, including the National Baptist Convention, USA. Dr. Williams' work has been featured in *Newsweek, The Washington Post, The Washington Times, Jet,* and *Ebony* Magazines as well as on CNN. As founder and president of Academic Resources Unlimited, Incorporated, he works to improve the quality of academic performance among youths and adults.

Two of Dr. Williams' books, *GROUNDED IN THE WORD* and *IT"S A READING THING: HELP YOUR CHILD UNDERSTAND* are found on www.youtube.com and www.christianbook.com. *GROUNDED IN THE WORD* has received positive reviews from Bishop T.D. Jakes, Bishop Eddie L. Long, and Pastors Paula White, Joyce Meyer, and Joel Osteen. Dr. Williams is a Partner of AARON"S ARMY of the T.D. Jakes Ministry. He resides in Upper Marlboro, MD with his wife, Dr. Mary H. Johnson who has coauthored books with him.

REQUEST FOR SPEAKING ENGAGEMENTS, MOTIVATIONAL AND VOCABULARY BUILDING WORKSHOPS

To:
Academic Resources Unlimited, Incorporated
P. O. Box 6745
Washington, D.C. 20020
(301) 768-8316
Educationissues@hotmail.com

Please contact me, my high school, church, or organization. You are needed as a motivational speker/workshop leader.

Name

School

Organization

Addess

Phone

E-mail

www.ingramcontent.com/pod-product-compliance
Lightning Source LLC
Chambersburg PA
CBHW071000040426
42443CB00007B/594